Guaranteed Ways to Make $100 A Day – Legally

by J. Doyle White

Images licensed by Fotolia.com unless otherwise noted.
Copyright © 2014 by J. Doyle White
All rights reserved. Published in the United States by J. Doyle White. First edition.
ISBN-13: 978-1500709860
ISBN-10: 1500709867

Table of Contents

Introduction..1

Do You Need a Business Plan?...............................4

Legalities of Running Your Own Business 5

How to Become Bonded, Licensed, and Insured......................................7

Scheduling and Organization 11

Marketing Yourself 13

ABOUT THE IDEAS BELOW................17

Working at the Client's Home or Business without a Truck......................19

Idea #1 - Vehicle Detailer......................20

   Step-by-Step on How to Be a Vehicle Detailer 23

Idea #2 - House Cleaner.......................30

   Step-by-Step on How to Be a House Cleaner 33

Idea #3 - Carpet Cleaner...................... 42

   Step-by-Step Instructions for Professional Carpet Cleaning............. 44

Idea #4 - House Sitter/Watcher............ 47

   Steps to Be a House Sitter/Watcher. 48

Idea #5 - Pet Sitter/Walker 51

   Steps to Be a Pet Sitter/Walker........ 53

Idea #6 - Home Help Aid 55

   Steps to Be a Home Help Aide........ 57

Idea #7 - Aquarium Maintenance 58

   Step-by-Step Instructions for Aquarium Maintenance 61

Going to Client's Home or Business with a Truck.68

   Idea #8 - Lawn Care Service............... 69

      Step-by-Step Basic Lawn Care Service 72

   Idea #9 - Professional Yard Sale......... 75

Step-by-Step in Running a Professional Yard Sale 77

Idea #10 - Trash Removal Service 82

Steps to Being a Professional Trash Removal Business 84

Idea #11 - Indoor Plant Care 86

Steps to Operating an Indoor Plant Care Business 88

Idea #12 - House Painter 91

Step-by-Step for Painting the Exterior of a Home 94

Step-by-Step for Painting the Interior of a Home 98

Idea #13 - Professional Handyman 102

Steps to Be a Professional Handyman 105

Idea #14 - Tree Cutting/Maintenance . 107

Steps to Be a Tree Cutter/Tree Maintainer (Arborist) 109

Ideas that Require Special Skills..........................…110

   Idea #15 - Outdoor Photographer 111

      Steps to Being an Outdoor Photographer 113

   Idea #16 - Baker/Cook 117

      Steps in Being a Baker/Cook 119

   Idea #17 - Seamstress 122

      Steps in Being a Seamstress 125

   Final Words 127

Introduction

You want to start your own business, you know you have the skills and experience it takes to do it, but you just need a little help getting there. Maybe you want to be your own boss but do not have a clue how to begin. The ideas in this book may help you to find just the job you need–and you can potentially start right now. All the jobs listed will help you to make at least $100 a day, legally, if you make the right connections.

Three sections of this book outline three different types of potential jobs. The first section is for jobs that take you to the client's home or business. These jobs do not require the use of a truck or trailer and can easily be done from any vehicle. The second section lists jobs that may require you to have a truck or at least a trailer. These jobs are tough, manual labor but are jobs you can start on your own.

The third section is short, and I call it the special skills section. Each job in this section requires that you have a preexisting skill, a sort of passion or hobby. You can take your hobby and turn it into a business which can net you $100 a day legally.

Whichever you choose, be sure to start off on the right foot. You will want to make sure your financial records are straight. You will need to look into being bonded, licensed, and insured where indicated. You may want to draw up a business plan to help gain potential investors and/or business loans to help grow the business. You may not need investors or loans; you may be able to run each of these businesses without that kind of help. But it is always nice to have that option should the need arise.

Do You Need a Business Plan?

While you may not think this will be a permanent job right now, you would be wise to write up a good business plan to back your intentions. If you ever want to obtain a business loan or look for investors, having this in place is absolutely imperative. If it sounds a bit cumbersome, do not fret. You can find fill-in-the-blank business plan builders online if you choose to go that route. You can also look on the SBA.gov website and find excellent advice on how to write a good business plan.

Legalities of Running Your Own Business

You want to retain all financial records and all receipts for proof of purchases and services. You will want to keep copies of income received. You may need to hire an accountant to help you with the taxes. When you are self-employed, there are a lot of different tax laws you must abide by. You need to consider that you will be paying self-employment taxes on state and federal tax returns. Because you won't have an employer to pay into Social Security, this is a part of what you will pay when you file your taxes. Keeping good records of everything you spend and earn will help your tax preparer to save you the most when it comes to filing your taxes. You can write off a percentage of the equipment, supplies, and expenses you have with your business, which will help. Talk with an accountant before you start, and set up a good filing system to keep all of your financial records.

How to Become Bonded, Licensed, and Insured

When you have a job that has you working out of someone else's home or business, you really need to become bonded, licensed, and insured. What this means is you will have all the proper permits and licenses you need to do such work–that you are legal. This will protect you should something occur while on the job. Without this, if you accidentally tear up something that belongs to the homeowner they can press a lawsuit against you. This is protection for both you and your client. It is a three-part process, and here is how you do it:

Becoming Bonded as an Independent Contractor

Some professions may not need to be bonded. Check with your local insurance agency to find out for sure. You may only need insurance, in which case you can skip this step. But if you need to be bonded, ask your insurance agency about the best company to acquire a surety bond. Please be aware that you may obtain one if your record is clean, meaning you have no criminal instances in your past. The bonding company will ask for financial records from the past year, so be sure to gather these prior to applying. If you use an accountant they can help you with this. Some companies may want up to three years' worth of records. If you are just starting out, talk with them about this, as some will work with you still if your criminal record is clear.

Each state is different, so you will need to call the licensing and regulations department of your state. Or if your state has an industry professional board (e.g., for a construction contractor) you can contact them. Some bonds are a "performance bond" and others are a "surety bond" and it all depends upon your line of work. You can always call the US Small Business Admin to ask for guidance with this (1-800-827-5722).

Acquiring a License

Again, the US Small Business Admin will help you with this. Contact them with the details of your type of business plan and they will direct you to the right place to obtain a license or a certification. You may be required to take a certification course in order to obtain a license. You may need to obtain licenses on state and federal, as well as local, levels. Again, this depends on the business and the state.

Acquiring Insurance

You can shop around with different insurance agencies to find the one who offers the best prices and services. You will want to insure for property and liability as well as work-related accidents and to insure your equipment if necessary. Once you find one that meets your needs, have the agency set up the policy. Make sure to keep this current.

Scheduling and Organization

If you are going to run a successful business, even if your business is to go mow lawns, you must maintain a sense of organization and stick with a schedule. If you do not grasp this in the beginning, you will run your business haphazardly. Success comes in waves of doing things the right way. Obtain a filing cabinet, an accordion box, or even just a plastic box with a lid to keep all your important papers regarding your business. Purchase a calendar or at least keep a good notebook to keep up with your appointments.

You want to keep receipts to everything you purchase for your business, including receipts for fuel to get to where you are going to perform the job. Keep a notebook to jot down ideas to help along the way. As you do your job, you are bound to come up with better ideas–ideas to streamline the work and ideas to add to the quality. Keep up with those by writing them down in a notebook. When you have time, you can go back and figure out ways of implementing them.

Keep a good schedule. Think about the timeframe it takes you to perform your jobs, and schedule your day accordingly. Many of the jobs may be a per-call basis, so if you are on a down time you can think of ways to market your job.

Marketing Yourself

When you are a freelancer going into business for yourself, you must market yourself. *You* are the brand. Your work is the quality (or lack thereof), and that's what will either propel you forward or hold you back. Knowing you are the brand, you must conduct yourself as a professional business owner. Even if you walk dogs or scrub toilets, do it as a professional. Be presentable. Don't show up for work in jeans that show your underwear or in shirts that are full of holes and never look like they saw a washing machine. You don't have to go out and buy a new wardrobe to cut trees, but you should be presentable. People will make a first-impression judgment on you. You want that first impression to be a good one. You want them to think, "Yeah, I will hire this person."

It's understandable that many of these jobs are dirty, and you will sweat and be dirty. People understand that too, but when you first walk onto a job site, be clean and presentable. You are selling your image first. Once they agree, you do the best job possible and keep the work on a professional level.

Being presentable and personable are the first steps in the marketing of your business, but you have other steps you must fulfill. How will people know you have a business? The second step involves calling all of your family and friends and letting them know you are open for business. Ask them nicely to refer you to others in need of your services. Word of mouth goes a long way in helping to build a business. Don't be shy here.

After talking with family and friends, you need to reach out to strangers. Depending upon your business, you should market yourself to the areas where you need to be. For example, if you are a home help aid you may approach businesses that cater to people who are in need of help. Perhaps go to the local health department and ask if you can leave your information in case they have patients who require home health aides. If you walk dogs, approach the veterinarians and leave your information. Do likewise with whatever job you offer.

The final step to marketing is to go out and advertise. Start with pinning flyers on your local store's bulletin boards. Create business cards and go to relevant businesses and ask if you can leave business cards for their patrons. Place small ads in the local newspaper. Also inquire about placing ads with their online services. See about placing a short ad on the local radio station. If your local community has websites, place ads with them as well. Without advertising, you will not reach as large an audience.

Keep up with the ads you place and see if you gain a return for them. If you don't, then don't do it again. If you do, keep advertising; it is paying off for you.

ABOUT THE IDEAS BELOW

For each idea, I give the target market. I do not want to come off as "sexist" so I will make it clear in the intro that "anyone" can do these jobs. But I make recommendations on the target market. For example, women are better suited for child care, while men are better for house painting. However either one can do the job just fine.

For each idea there are:

- Targeted people
- The education or skills needed to perform the job
- Where to perform the job
- The equipment needed to perform the job
- Details about any legalities that may surround such a job if relevant
- Steps to perform the job

- Ideas about fees charged for the jobs (this will vary but we can give guesstimates)
- Any other pertinent information you will need to "get started" with the job

Working at the Client's Home or Business without a Truck

The 7 ideas below are jobs that will require you to go to the client's home or business. These jobs do not require you to have a truck, though having one for a couple of the jobs may be easier. The jobs are detail-oriented and will require you to have knowledge beforehand. If you wish to go into any of these jobs, you need to either know what you are doing through experience and education or you will need to educate yourself first. The better you can do these jobs, the more income you can potentially earn.

Idea #1 – Vehicle Detailer

Vehicle detailing is a very in-demand job. People love their vehicles to shine and sparkle but few enjoy taking the time to clean and detail them. You can work this job right on your own property if you have a good area to park vehicles and access to a water faucet. It is possible to take the work to the client, if their vehicle is parked in an area suitable for detail work. Ideally it would be nice to pull the vehicle into a garage to detail the inside and then pull it to an area outside to detail the exterior.

Target Group: Young adults, men, and women.

Education and Skills Needed: You do not need a formal education to be a vehicle detailer, but you do need to know how to properly clean the vehicle. YouTube is rich in tutorials to show you how to detail any part of the vehicle. Ask your local vehicle dealerships if you can observe the process. Also read up on it on the internet. And the best way to gain skills is to practice. Detail your own vehicle. Ask your family and friends if you can detail theirs. Take photos along the way to document the process. You will learn best here by simply doing the job.

Where: Detailing a vehicle can be done right from your home, *if* you have an area to do it. You need plenty of space to park a vehicle and a water hydrant. You also need an electrical outlet nearby for the vacuum cleaner. You can also offer to go to the client if they have the above available.

Equipment Needed: buckets, sponges, rags, towels, car paint safe soap, tire cleaner, window cleaner, car interior cleaner, vacuum, car polish, headlight/taillight polish, engine degreaser, water hose, hose sprayer, steam cleaner, leather upholstery cleaner, fabric upholstery cleaner, carpet cleaner, bags, gloves, chamois cloths, terry cloths, toothbrushes, cotton swabs, whitewall tire cleaner, and tire dressing.

Where to Purchase the Equipment: You can find the above items at a store like Walmart or at a specialty automotive store like O'Reilly's, Napa, or AutoZone. You can even find good deals online at stores like Amazon.com.

Step-by-Step on How to Be a Vehicle Detailer

What to Do: Detailing a vehicle means taking great care with every aspect of the vehicle. Using the right cleaning agents and equipment will help you to do a better job. Vehicle focus areas: cleaning and polishing the paint; cleaning the bumpers and wheels; cleaning the tires; cleaning and polishing the headlights, taillights, and other lights; detailing the interior; cleaning the dash; cleaning the steering wheel (making sure you do not use some oily, slick agent); steaming the carpets; cleaning the upholstery; cleaning the windows; and lastly, cleaning the engine bay (carefully).

Step One - Start with the vehicle interior. Take everything that is not a part of the interior out of the vehicle. Since you are doing this for a client, be neat and methodical about it. This is where you will gather your zipper bags and carefully place all the loose items within the bags, marking on them where you got the belongings (front console tray, passenger side door, etc.). Remove the floor mats.

Step Two - Vacuum the interior. Use the attachments on your vacuum cleaner and go to work. Vacuum the dust off the dashboard and work your way from top to bottom on the interior. Remember to vacuum all the nooks and crannies. Move the seats forward and backward and vacuum the floors.

Step Three - Use a quality vehicle stain remover to clean any stains on the carpets or upholstery. If the carpet and upholstery is very dirty, you may want to do a shampoo with a quality vehicle foaming cleaner. Read the instructions on the cleaner for best results. Repeat until the carpets and upholstery are clean and as stain free as possible. If the interior has leather, clean it with the appropriate leather cleaner; never use a vinyl cleaner on leather. If you are in doubt, always ask your client to point out any leather. Never over-saturate the fabric or carpet with the cleaner. Using a foam cleaner helps to keep this from occurring.

Step Four - Wash the floor mats. If they are vinyl or rubber, just spray with a hose. If they are very dirty, use a little vehicle soap and water and be sure to rinse. Dry with a towel and set aside.

Step Five - Using a mild cleaner (you may find some just for vehicle interiors or use an all-purpose cleanser), wipe all the hard surfaces. Use vinyl cleaner for vinyl areas. Do not put a "high gloss" conditioner on vinyl or leather seats and certainly not on the steering wheel. Spray a vehicle interior "protectant" spray (like Armor All®) and wipe with a soft cloth. Or use wipes that come in a container. Use cotton swabs and soft toothbrushes to clean around buttons and knobs and insets such as the air vents.

Step Six - Clean the interior windows with a good glass cleaner. Ask your client if they have an "aftermarket" tint on any of their windows; if they do, wash the window with a spritz of seltzer water and a crumpled newspaper. Otherwise, use either a soft, clean cloth or paper towels to wipe the windows.

Step Seven - Wash the exterior of the vehicle. Park the vehicle in the shade if possible. Spray the entire exterior with water. Pour the right amount (look on the bottle for directions) of car-safe or "carwash" soap into a bucket. Use a large sponge and apply soap water in gentle scrubbing motions all over the vehicle's exterior surface.

Step Eight - Dry the exterior with a chamois cloth. This helps to keep water spots from forming and gives it an extra shine.

Step Nine - Wash the wheels. Use a brush and cleaners that are made specifically for wheels. If the rims are shiny chrome, use a glass cleaner to shine them.

Step Ten - Now you are ready for the polish or wax. Here is where you do not want to skimp with a bargain formula. Quality is best because it will leave the vehicle looking so good your client will want to come back. Read and follow the directions on the polish/wax. Only wax the painted area of the exterior and do not get it on the rubber trim or windows. If you do get wax or polish on these areas, use a toothbrush or cotton swab and spray with a vehicle-safe cleaner (like you used on the interior) and gently rub the wax or polish off. Buff as described in the directions.

Step Eleven - Open the hood of the vehicle. Spray the engine with an engine-safe cleanser and then rinse with a gentle mist of the water hose. You can use a rubber/vinyl protectant spray for those areas to give it an extra sparkle, if desired.

Step Twelve - Clean the tires with a "whitewall" tire cleaner. Once cleaned, finish with a coat of tire dressing and wipe off with a clean cloth, making sure the tires are completely dry before driving.

How Much You Can Earn: This is dependent upon your location and upon the size of the vehicle. Normal car detailing services can cost from $50 to $150 or higher per detailing. Adjust the fee according to the services ordered and products requested. Have on hand bargain- and high-quality vehicle cleaning products and let your client choose.

You can easily earn $100 or more a day doing this work. You can also work with the local vehicle repair and body shops and dealerships.

Idea #2 – House Cleaner

This is an age-old job that still gives great opportunities for many hundreds of thousands of people around the world today. A house cleaner can have as little or as much work as they want and will have no problems in keeping their business going strong. Some people may desire for light housework daily, while others may opt for a weekly or monthly cleaning. Ideally you can target more affluent areas and resort towns. People who have vacation homes often hire house cleaners to come in before they are due to arrive. Who wants to arrive to a dirty home? Timeshare properties are another area to look at for clients, as these properties are constantly receiving new guests. Retired areas are also a great place to find clients, as retired folks travel often and perhaps they just want to relax and not deal with the grind of a good house cleaning. You can also offer your services to companies with apartment and house rentals.

Target Group: Women, men, and young adults.

Education and Skills Needed: You do not need formal education to be a house cleaner; you just need to know how to clean all the rooms and areas properly. The best way to gain skills is to do it. Clean your own home, acting as if you are cleaning it for a client. Go to YouTube and find video tutorials on how to clean the house. House cleaning isn't hard, it just requires attention to detail.

Where: At the client's home or business.

Equipment Needed: Household cleaning supplies: broom, mop, vacuum, window cleaner, bathroom cleaner, kitchen cleaner, floor cleaner, duster, dusting spray, carpet powder, mold/mildew killer, toilet cleaner, dustpan, gloves, buckets, sponges, rags, towels, scrub brush for toilet, scrubber, and mops for hardwood floors and other non-carpet surfaces.

Step-by-Step on How to Be a House Cleaner
What to Do: Detail cleaning of the home or business. Start in the front or back room and work your way through. Clean the floors–vacuum and mop all surfaces and baseboards; detail the faucets, tubs, showers, and sinks; clean the windows, toilets, ceiling fans, doorknobs, doors, and porch.

Step One - Dust. Grab a duster or a dry cloth and dusting spray and hit all the surfaces where dust can rest in all rooms but the kitchen and bathrooms. Remove the items from surfaces, spray dusting spray, and wipe with the dry cloth. For places that can't be sprayed directly, use a duster. Items to dust include all tables, nightstands, mantels, ceiling fans, window ledges, baseboards, picture frames, decorative items, and any other "dusty" surface. Be sure to replace all the times that were moved.

Step Two - Bathroom cleaning. The first thing you want to do is remove all items to allow free room to clean. Bathrooms are one of the dirtiest rooms in the home, so extra care is needed to clean and disinfect. Start with the mirrors. Clean with a good window cleaner; spray first and wipe with either paper towels or a clean, dry towel. Next, clean the vanity. If the surfaces in the bathroom are very dirty, you may need a bucket of water and some strong cleanser. If they are not so dirty, a spray on cleaner will work just fine. Clean all the surfaces, starting with the faucet fixtures, the surface of the countertop, then the sink. Next, do the same for the bathtub or shower. You may need to apply soap scum remover or mildew remover. Make sure you use the appropriate cleanser for the tub because fiberglass tubs need a non-abrasive cleanser. Use a sponge mop if the tub or shower is too hard to reach. Be sure to rinse the sponge often. Next, clean the outside of the toilet bowl, seat, lid, tank, and all areas of it. Clean with the same cleanser used on the vanity and sink. After the outside is sparkling, add a toilet bowl cleanser inside a "flushed" toilet. Scrub the entire toilet bowl with a toilet bowl brush, including under the rim. Allow the water to sit for at least 10 minutes before flushing. Be sure to run a cleaning cloth over the walls and baseboards. Lastly, apply a damp mop to the floor and mop the entire surface.

Step Three - Haul out the vacuum cleaner. Go through the house and pick up the clutter on the carpets and rugs. Remove any loose items from the furniture. Starting with the furniture, place the upholstery attachment to the vacuum and vacuum all the furniture, including lifting the seat cushions and vacuuming underneath. Run the attachment over lamp shades. Ask the client if they wish to use carpet powder. If they do, sprinkle the powder on all the carpets and rugs and wait about 15 minutes before vacuuming. Some people do not like this, so offer it to each client and carry through with their wishes. Where easily done, move furniture to vacuum underneath. This is not a steaming job, so don't worry if it's too big a piece to move. Don't hurt your back. You will need to vacuum all the rugs and carpets after vacuuming the furniture. Be sure to vacuum around the hearth, fireplace, and/or wood stoves. Open closets and remove the items on the floor and vacuum in there. Vacuum the tracks on patio or sliding glass doors as well.

Step Four - Kitchen cleaning. This is a big, detailed job. Start with the refrigerator. Using an all-purpose kitchen cleaner, spray the exterior of the fridge and wipe with a clean, dry cloth. Remember to wipe down the top as well. Do the same for the freezer.

Step Five - Oven cleaning. Take special care with the oven by using the appropriate oven cleaner. Follow the instructions on the cleaner, which probably includes removing any debris in the bottom of the oven first. Use newspaper to catch any drip from the oven cleaner on the floor. If the oven is self-cleaning, follow the instructions for cleaning it.

Step Six - Wipe down all the small appliances with an all-purpose kitchen cleaner and a clean dry cloth. This includes toasters, coffee makers, microwaves, etc. For the interior of the microwave, fill a microwave-proof cup with water and place it inside to cook for five minutes. Allow it to sit in the closed microwave for an additional 10 minutes, and then wipe with a clean, dry cloth. Remove and wash the carousal plate.

Step Seven - Wipe out the inside of the dishwasher using a clean, damp cloth. Remove and clean the silverware trays in hot, soapy water.

Step Eight - Clean the sink. Use a clean toothbrush to scrub all the crevices that surround it and around the faucets. Use dish liquid and a sponge or rag and wash the entire sink and then rinse with clean water. Use a clean, dry towel to dry and shine it.

Step Nine - Mop all the floors according to the type. Hardwood floors require a special wood soap and a shine. A solution of equal vinegar and water works well on any other floor surface; ask the owner if they have a preference. Start at the far end of a room and mop your way to the exit. Run fans to help dry the floors if available.

Step Ten - Using a sponge or rag and an all-purpose cleanser, or a "Magic Eraser," clean all the cabinet doors and drawers. Especially focus on the area around the knob/handle and the lower doors and drawers where spills are likely to occur.

Step Eleven - Scrub the baseboards in the kitchen with an all-purpose cleaner (or a cleaner fit for the surface). Kitchens are notorious for messy baseboards; take extra care to make the room shine.

Step Twelve - Clean the vent-a-hood with all-purpose kitchen cleaner and a clean, dry cloth. Remove the filter and soak in hot water and use a toothbrush and dish soap to remove any grime. Dry with a towel and allow to air dry before replacing. Be sure to shine up the light cover as well.

Step Thirteen - Take time to clean and disinfect all the doorknobs in the home. Spray with a disinfectant spray and wipe clean. Wipe up any smudges or prints off the door.

Step Fourteen - Clean and shine the windows with a good window cleaner and clean, dry cloths. Wipe down the window ledges. Don't forget to clean any windows on doors as well.

How Much You Can Earn: Base fees start around $75 for a small home or apartment and go up depending on the size of the home. You can charge by the square foot of the home or by the amount of time it takes to do a thorough cleaning job. Charge $50-75 an hour or $15 per square foot. You can adjust this according to the going rates in your local area.

Idea #3 – Carpet Cleaner

Not too many people enjoy shampooing or steaming their carpets. But you may be motivated to like it if you were getting paid to do it, right? Any home or business with carpets is a potential client for a carpet cleaner. The key is to have quality equipment and a good back. This is physical labor and you will have to put some muscle into it. Even if you don't have a truck and you haul your equipment in the back seat of your car, you have to haul the equipment from the vehicle to the home or business and back again. Stay in good shape to do a good job as a professional carpet cleaner.

Target Group: Strong women and men.

Education and Skills Needed: You do not need formal education to learn how to clean carpets; you can learn by watching videos found on the internet. Just do a search for "How to professionally clean carpets." There are varying levels of what you can do for carpet cleaning. The steps below outline the basics you will need. Practice on your own carpets. Ask family and friends if you can practice on their carpets. This may be "free" work, but the experience is invaluable and you will learn how to do a better job for paying clients by practicing first.

Where: At the location of the client.

Equipment Needed: Professional-style carpet cleaner/steamer, carpet cleaner made for your carpet cleaning machine— different formulas (one for allergens, pets, and odors), spot removers, professional-style vacuum cleaner with attachments, and fans.

Step-by-Step Instructions for Professional Carpet Cleaning

What to Do: Follow the step-by-step instructions below.

Step One - Remove all the furniture from the carpet area. If need be, enlist the help of a partner to move heavier pieces. Make sure to have permission from the home or business owner to move the furniture. Offer a discount if they will have it out of the way before you arrive.

Step Two - Vacuum the carpet, making sure to cover the entire floor. Running the vacuum twice, after changing the bag or emptying the bucket, is smart.

Step Three - Follow the instructions on the carpet cleaning machine, and add the right amount of water and cleaning solution. Run the cleaner over the carpet in the method specified by the carpet cleaner manufacturer.

Step Four: If you see any stains, use stain remover as per the bottle's instructions.

Step Five: Run the carpet cleaner over the area another time or two until all the high-traffic areas are erased and the carpet looks brand new.

Step Six: If there are ceiling fans, turn them on high. If not, set up fans in the doorways and turn on high to help dry.

Step Seven: Replace all the furniture as you originally found it.

How Much You Can Earn: Generally, as of 2014, professional carpet cleaners are charging around $45 average per room.

When a client calls for service, you can go to their home or business and evaluate the rooms; if a room is twice as large as an average 100 square feet, you can charge more. If there is extra heavy furniture you need to move, charge more. Offer a discount if they will do all the heavy lifting before you arrive. If you consider an average home has at least 3 to 5 rooms, you can easily earn $135 to $180 per job. If you do 2 jobs a day, that's close to $400 a day.

Idea #4 – House Sitter/Watcher

A house sitter or watcher is a person who will either drop by or stay at a home while the owners are away. The most popular version is a watcher or someone who will come by the home or business at specified times to check in on things.

Target Group: Anyone who is leaving their home unattended for an extended time.

Education and Skills Needed: You do not need any formal education or training in order to do this job. All that is required is the ability to go to the home, walk in, and check on things.

Where: At the client's home.

Equipment Needed: None.

Steps to Be a House Sitter/Watcher

What to Do: Make a pre-determined plan with the homeowner as to how often you will come by the home. Most homeowners will want you to go by the house daily or every other day.

Your duties may include:

- Watering plants
- Feeding pets
- Checking to make sure the water, electricity, and/or gas is okay
- Making sure no one has broken into the home
- Make sure all doors and windows are closed
- Maybe switching around which lights stay on all night to make it look as if someone is home
- Picking up mail

- Light house cleaning (like dusting, running the dishwasher, etc.)

In some cases, the owner may want someone staying on the property at all times.

How Much You Can Earn: The general going rate for house sitting is $30 to $50 a day for just going by and checking on things. It's at least $50+ a day to stay overnight. Reasons to charge a larger fee include taking care of pets, doing house cleaning, and meeting someone for an appointment (like lawn work or termite control), distance to the home, etc. If you line up 3 or 4 clients at once, the earnings potential here are well over $100 a day. For people leaving on lengthy extended stays you can work out a weekly or monthly fee.

Get clients by advertising you have this service. Advertise on the local radio, in the local newspaper, and on store bulletin boards.

Idea #5 – Pet Sitter/Walker

Just like little children, pets sometimes need a sitter. Whether you have the pets in your care or your job is to leash 'em up and walk them, you will be busy.

Target Group: Men and women.

Education and Skills Needed: Being a pet sitter/walker does need some skills. First and foremost, you must be an animal lover. If you do not enjoy being around animals, you will not do a good job with pet walking and sitting. You can obtain certifications on walking animals and on pet sitting. Do an internet search for such things and you will find websites that offer courses to help you achieve these certifications. The certification is not necessary to do the job, but if you have it you may receive more work with pet owners.

Guaranteed Ways to Make $100 Today - Legally

Where: At the owner's home or business or at your home.

Equipment Needed: Kennels, leashes, and food dishes.

Steps to Be a Pet Sitter/Walker

What to Do: This is basically an easy job. It is best done by someone who loves animals. If you don't like dogs or cats then do not offer to do this job.

Basically, as a dog sitter/walker you have several different scenarios you can offer:

- Walk the dog. This normally takes about 25 to 30 minutes. You will go to the dog owner's home and leash the dog and take them for a half hour walk. You may be asked to do this daily, a couple of times a day, or a couple of times a week.
- Pet sit. You will either come to the dog (or cat) owner's home or they will drop the animal off with you. You will then watch the dog (or cat) for however many hours needed. During the time you are watching

the dog you will need to take it outside for walks.

How Much You Can Earn: $15-20 per visit for "dog walking." Pet sitting you will need to calculate an hourly rate comparable to what real babysitters earn. This can be anywhere from $10 an hour to $150 per week if you keep the dog for several hours each day. Of course, you will make the bulk of your income if you gather several different clients. If you have 5 to 10 clients whose dogs you walk each day, that can be upwards of $200 a day.

Find out from your local veterinarians if there are "dog sitting" or "dog walking" certification programs around. If you have a certification you can charge a larger fee.

Idea #6 – Home Help Aid

A home help aid is not to be confused with a "home health aide." You will not be required to do anything regarding health but more so with helping with everyday, basic homemaking. Some people are invalids, sickly, or just unable to get up and do their basic daily house tasks. As a home help aid, you may need to drive your client to the doctor or help to pick up the house or cook a meal. Whatever the task, it will be basic, everyday things that people need help doing.

Target Group: Women mostly do this, but it is suitable for men too.

Education and Skills Needed: You need basic skills in home making. You need to have good people skills, too. This job will have you also being a "visitor" to the person who you are helping. You need to be personable. You need to be willing to happily help out with whatever basic tasks the homeowner will have for you.

Where: At the client's home.

Equipment Needed: This can range from just sitting and visiting with the person to basic housecleaning supplies to cooking supplies.

Steps to Be a Home Help Aide

What to Do: A home help aid is just someone who goes to the client's home and helps with basic homemaking tasks. Generally, you will offer to help the person do light housework, cook meals, do light yard work, or whatever they may need help with. Basically, you will be helping them with basic house making tasks. This is not the same as a home health care worker, where they are required to administer medications, baths, and other physical things concerning their health.

How Much You Can Earn: Typically, you can charge anywhere from $20 to $50 an hour, depending on what you are required to do and the area in which you live. If you have three to five clients lined up per day, you can easily earn around $100 a day.

Idea #7 – Aquarium Maintenance

If you are knowledgeable about aquariums and enjoy working with fish, you can start a business providing maintenance for clients with aquariums. It may help if you take the initiative and learn all you can about aquarium care and maintenance. Not all aquariums are alike. You need to familiarize yourself with what fish can go together and with the maintenance of freshwater and saltwater aquariums.

Target Group: Men and women.

Education and Skills Needed: While you do not need a "formal" education to do aquarium maintenance, you do need to know your craft. The only people who do this sort of job should have excellent knowledge in how to maintain both fresh- and saltwater aquariums. Read books on aquariums and freshwater and saltwater fish care. Learn what fish can go together and what need to be separated. Visit your local pet supply store, particularly a store with aquariums, and ask if they have training sessions on aquarium care. You can find good books at these stores as well as online. As with everything else listed in this book, the best way to know how to do this is to practice. If you plan to offer maintenance for both fresh- and saltwater aquariums, you should have the set ups in your own home. You need to know firsthand what you are doing. If you don't have them and have family or friends with these tanks, ask them if you can provide the maintenance free of charge to give you good experience with it. Have a way of figuring out solutions to issues should they arise, such as a manual or a knowledgeable person.

Where: At the business or home where the aquarium is located.

Equipment Needed: siphons; several (5 gallon, 2 gallon, and 1 gallon) buckets with lids; towels; plastic tarps; nets; algae pads; tongs; saltwater test kits; clamps; faucet adapter; razor scraper; specimen container; knife; coral epoxy; carbon pellets; filter media bags; gravel vacuum; zip ties; test kits for ammonia, Ca, KH, Mg, nitrate, nitrite, pH, and phosphate; filter pads and media; cord labels; vinegar-based, aquarium-safe glass cleaner; salt mix; refractometer; thermometer; and chlorine remover.

Step-by-Step Instructions for Aquarium Maintenance

What to Do: Aquarium maintenance for clients entails mostly cleaning the inside of the aquarium while making sure the fish are not harmed. This is a big undertaking, which is why people will hire it.

Before you ever start a job, have a terms and agreement for the client to sign. Be sure to put in the terms that you will not be liable for any leaks or damage that occurs after you have cleaned the tank. Explain that there will always be a risk of leaks in maintaining an aquarium.

Before you begin any new job, label each cord properly so when you need to remove one you will know exactly where it belongs when you replace it.

Saltwater Tanks

Step One - Because of the complexity of saltwater aquariums, you need to prepare the water the night before. Star with distilled water and pour the amount you will need into clean buckets. Use an aquarium heater to heat the water to the temperature it needs to be. Pour in the salt mixture (you can purchase the pre-measured salt at pet stores). The salt mix should have instructions on the package as to the amount per gallon of water. Place an air stone connected to a small pump in the water to aerate it. Before you use the water, be sure to check the salinity by using a refractometer. The reading should be around 1.025. The temperature needs to be in the upper 70s Fahrenheit.

Step Two - A saltwater tank will need prepared saltwater, however much you think you will need to replace once you clean the tank.

Step Three - Before you siphon the water, take an algae pad and scrub the algae from the sides of the tank. Use a razor scraper to remove tough algae areas.

Step Four - Saltwater tanks require that at least 10 % of the water be changed out at least twice a month. Doing this helps to keep the nitrates down. Siphon out 10% of the water in the tank into one of the larger buckets you have.

Step Five - Using the gravel vacuum, gently vacuum the gravels by pushing it through. This will help to loosen the fish waste and old food to be suctioned into the hose. Be sure to keep the hose end away from small fish. If there is sand, you can hold the vacuum in the water about an inch or two to gather the debris and not disturb the sand.

Step Six - Remove the aquarium decorations and wipe down with an algae pad. If the stains are tough, use a clean, soft-bristled toothbrush. If the stains are set in, create a solution of 1 part bleach to 9 parts water and soak for about 10 to 15 minutes. Rinse with boiling water. Allow to air dry before returning to the tank.

Step Seven - Clean off the crusty salt residue at the top of the aquarium with an algae pad. This is called "salt creep."

Step Eight - Pour the prepared saltwater from step one into the tank to replace the water siphoned out.

Freshwater Tanks

Step One - Take an algae pad and clean the sides of the aquarium. For tough spots, use a razor scraper, otherwise just an algae pad to wipe the sides of the tank.

Step Two - Siphon out about 15% of the water. If the fish are ill, siphon out at least half of the water.

Step Three - Vacuum the gravel by placing the end of the aquarium vacuum into the gravels. You may use a filter over the opening to avoid sucking up small fish. For sand, stick the vacuum about an inch into the water and suck up debris. Gently rake the top of the sand with your fingers to loosen any debris.

Step Four - Remove all the decorations and clean them using an algae pad. If they are very stained, loosen with a clean, soft-bristled toothbrush and wash in a bleach solution (1 part bleach to 9 parts water; soak for up to 15 minutes) and rinse with boiling water. Allow to air dry before replacing back into the tank.

Step Five - Add tap water to a clean bucket and try to make it the same temperature as what's in the tank. Treat the water with chlorine remover according to the treatment bottle's instructions. Replace the water in the tank.

Step Six - Wipe down the outside of the tank and hood with a clean, damp cloth. Do not use "cleaners" on it. Only vinegar-based solutions are safe.

Step Seven - Make sure the filter is changed at least once a month. At the very least, remove it and rinse it under tap water before replacing.

How Much You Can Earn: Generally you can charge around $60 an hour for aquarium maintenance. Businesses may hire you to come in weekly to keep their aquarium looking pristine. Home owners may hire you to come by monthly to do a thorough cleaning. It can take a couple of hours to do a job, so potentially you can earn at least $180 per job. If you could have at least 5 clients a week you can earn close to $50,000 a year.

Going to Client's Home or Business with a Truck

These business ideas will require you to have a truck or at least a vehicle with a trailer because you will be hauling around lawn care equipment. You may need both a truck and a trailer if you are hauling a riding lawn mower. You will need a way to get the mower off the truck easily.

Idea #8 – Lawn Care Service

If you are physically able and love the outdoors, you can provide a lawn care service. This type of work is not for the faint of heart. This is genuine, hard work—labor intensive—and it can be very rewarding and lucrative. The needed equipment is pricey, but you can find used lawn equipment until you can afford to buy new.

Target Group: Physically strong men and women.

Education and Skills Needed: You do not need "formal" education to offer lawn care services, but you certainly need to know what you are doing. Learn all you can through manuals, books, and even YouTube videos on proper lawn care maintenance. Not only do you need to know how to mow the lawn and care for it properly, you need to know how to maintain your equipment. You must do things to your equipment, such as lawn mower, weed eater, and any others with engines. Just like a car needs maintenance like oil changes and such, so will your lawn care equipment. Keep up with the care of the equipment and either learn how to do the maintenance yourself or take the equipment to a professional. If you don't properly maintain the equipment, it will not operate at top performance. The manuals that come with the equipment will have a maintenance schedule. Follow this schedule. If you purchase your equipment used then you should call a small engines repair shop and ask their advice on maintenance of such equipment. Again, practice on your own lawn. Remember you are the brand. If you want people to know you do a good job with lawn care then your own lawn should look pristine. If you don't have lawn, ask to do the lawn of family and friends to give you practice. Experience is the best education.

Where: Home and business owners with lawns that need maintenance.

Equipment Needed: Lawnmower (both a push mower and a riding mower with the ability to pick up the cut grass), a weed eater, a patio edger, hoes, rakes, shovels, large lawn bags, a water hose, sprinklers, fertilizer, grass seed, weed and feed, weed whackers, hedge trimmers (both electric and manual), and a leaf blower.

Step-by-Step Basic Lawn Care Service

What to Do: The general idea with lawn care is to manicure lawns and give them curb appeal. The most basic work is cutting the grass, but it actually goes way beyond that.

Step One - Clear the lawn area from any debris, such as rocks, twigs, toys, lawn furniture, or anything that can hurt the lawn mower or that the lawn mower can hurt.

Step Two - Mow the lawn. Be mindful if anyone steps into the yard or if a vehicle drives by. You do not want to throw a stick or rock to hurt anyone.

Step Three - Run the weed eater in areas where the lawn mower couldn't reach.

Step Four - Use a hoe or shears to finish weeding around hedges and flowers.

Step Five - Use a patio edger to edge around patios, porches, and driveways.

Step Six - Trim the hedges and bushes.

Step Seven - If you don't have an attachment vacuum on the lawn mower, go back and use a rake to rake up all the cut grass and weeds to dispose of in a large trash lawn bag.

Step Eight - If the owner wishes, water the freshly-cut lawn and surrounding flowers, trees, and hedges.

Extra Services for Lawn Care Maintenance
For extra fees you can offer to fertilize the lawn, do weed and feed, and plant winter grass. The type of fertilizer will depend on the type of grass and soil your client has. You need to familiarize yourself with the

soil types in your area and determine the best fertilizers.

How Much You Can Earn: $40 an hour up to over $60 an hour, depending on the amount of work needed. For example, if there is a lot of weed eating, hedge trimming, and care around flowerbeds, then you can charge more than you would for just straight mowing. Normally it takes 2 to 3 hours to mow an average yard, netting you around $100 per job. Of course, it will be less for smaller yards and more for larger yards. Word of mouth does very well with professional lawn care businesses. Place a magnetic sign on the side of the truck and advertise what you do in the local papers and on store bulletin boards.

Idea #9 – Professional Yard Sale

A professional yard sale business is very diversified. You need to have a place to hold the yard sale and you must have a truck in order to make purchases for the yard sale. The diversity comes in the items you will handle as well as where you will sell them.

Target Group: Anyone with a truck and the ability to gather large and small items.

Education and Skills Needed: There is no formal education required for doing yard sales professionally. A good knowledge of finances and sales is helpful. You can take courses to help you with your salesman (person) abilities. You just need to jump in and start doing this. The best place to start is in your own home or garage. You can also ask family and friends if they plan to have a yard sale and ask if you can help with it to gain experience.

Where: Yard sales can be done at a number of different locations:

- In your yard or garage
- Rent a booth at a flea market
- Rent a storage unit and sell from the unit
- Participate in parking lot sales
- Participate with other organizations; offer a percentage of your profits, for example, at a church bazaar, alongside a car wash, etc.

Equipment Needed: A truck and a dolly, money box or bag and change, tables to set up smaller items, and a chair for you.

Step-by-Step in Running a Professional Yard Sale

What to Do: The steps in this vary according to what you purchase and what you sell. Anything is good to offer for sale. You can sell clothes, furniture, household items, gardening items, craft items—anything. Make sure you have the proper permits from your town to run such a business. Some towns require them while others do not.

Step One - You need items to sell. At first you can clean out your home, your attic, and your garage. Get rid of any item you don't want. Start with a yard sale at your home.

Step Two - If you don't have many items of your own to sell, start by looking at the thrift stores like Goodwill or the Salvation Army. Purchase items that you feel you can resell for more than your purchase price.

Step Three - While this may seem counterintuitive, you need to visit other yard sales. Many yard sale "professionals" will peruse the local yard and garage sales to look for cheap finds they can offer for sale later in their own sales. You can stop by early in the morning and offer a set amount for "the whole lot"—say $250 or whatever your best guess is. Some people will go ahead and sell all to a pro like this. Another time to stop by is near the end, when things are practically given away. Collect your goods bargaining for the lowest prices.

Step Four - Keep your ears open for when people give away items. You can find all sorts of items, including furniture, that's "Yours for the taking." Often, people just want to get rid of big, bulky items if someone will come haul it away for them. These are good for your "yard" sale.

Step Five - Have you ever heard of dumpster diving? This is a way to find goods you can resell. People will throw away perfectly good items, including big pieces like furniture. Many pros find excellent items to sell and make a profit in the dumpster or at the curb.

Step Six - Advertise where and when you plan to have your "yard" sale. Pros normally have set times for the sales, depending on the location. If you are doing an actual yard sale, treat it like any other yard sale. Set a time, preferably surrounding the weekends. Advertise in the local paper and on bulletin boards at stores. If you are doing a flea market booth, you can advertise your hours of business. If you are doing it out of a storage unit, you can advertise the hours you will be there or you can advertise a phone number for people to call you to come by and look at the items. In the ads, list the items you will have for sale.

Step Seven - Be smart with your earnings. In order to make money in this business, you need to continually reinvest in purchasing and acquiring "new" items. You need to keep aside funds for fees for the ads and permits and rental fees if applicable.

How Much You Can Earn: The earnings depend on the items you sell and the profit margin. Skilled yard sale professionals can earn several hundred dollars a day if they have the right items. The key is to have items that people want. Furniture is always a hit. Find a need and fill it.

Guaranteed Ways to Make $100 Today - Legally

Idea #10 – Trash Removal Service

One thing about this business is that everyone will be in need of it at some point. We must deal with our trash or it will overwhelm our homes and businesses. While trash service is available in most places, it is generally limited to a certain number of garbage bags. There are times when other items need to be hauled off and unless you have a truck it can be a difficult task. There are locations that may not have trash service; in this case a trash removal service will be very handy indeed.

Target Group: Strong men and women.

Education and Skills Needed: You do not need formal education to run a trash removal service. You do need to be in good shape. Learn the proper ways of lifting, and lift to keep from hurting your back.

Where: At the home or business of your client.

Equipment Needed: A truck or trailer is vital, as well as shovels, rakes, garbage cans, and trash bags of all sizes.

Steps to Being a Professional Trash Removal Business

What to Do: Find people and businesses that need trash hauled off. Target residential areas with the offer to haul off what the regular trash service doesn't. Target construction sites and offer to haul off the garbage that collects as they build.

Step One - Have a good truck or trailer and the equipment above. Put a magnetic sign on the side of the truck advertising your trash removal business. Place ads in the local papers. Bring brochures to local construction companies and businesses.

Step Two - Schedule times to pick up trash to haul with your clients. Your clientele may change often, so be prepared for your daily schedule to be different.

Step Three - Pick up the trash, which may range from a few trash bags to old appliances and furniture and other odd items from construction sites.

Step Four - Haul the trash to the local dump. If you have recycling centers, you may offer to haul to these places.

How Much You Can Earn: When coming up with your fees, find out what your local dump charges per truckload as well as the gas and maintenance on your truck, and adjust your fee according to that. You should charge enough that you walk away with at least $30 per hour for your work. If you just work 3 to 4 hours a day, you will hit over $100 a day.

Idea #11 – Indoor Plant Care

As a professional offering indoor plant care services, you will want a truck to haul around potting soil, extra plants, and your equipment. This business mainly caters to other businesses that enjoy having live plants in their offices. You may have clients in homes of people who are just too busy to deal with live plants but who like having the live plants in the home. You must have a green thumb in order to this job well.

Target Group: Women and men.

Education and Skills Needed: While you don't need a formal education to run an indoor plant care business, it wouldn't hurt to take courses in horticulture. This will help you to better know how to care for the plants. You do need knowledge about how to care for indoor plants properly. You do need a "green thumb," meaning you enjoy caring for and growing plants and plants thrive under your care.

Where: At the client's home or business.

Equipment Needed: Truck or trailer, potting soil, plant food, fertilizer, spray bottles of water, small shovels, garden trowel, pocket snips, plastic saucers, pest and fungus control spray, and whitefly traps.

Steps to Operating an Indoor Plant Care Business

What to Do: The steps to caring for indoor plants vary according to the plant. You need to make it a top priority to know your plants. You need to know how often to water, how much sunlight they need, how much plant food and fertilizers to use, and the type of pests and funguses that can attack.

Step One - Evaluate the plants your client has. Make a determination as to how often you need to visit to maintain the plants.

Step Two - Carry all the equipment you need and go to your businesses and homes to care for the plants. Keep a good log book of what you've done on each visit.

Step Three - Leave any instructions with your plant owner, but keep in mind they hire you to make it maintenance free for them. If the plant needs to be fed or fertilized before your next return, implement the right kind of system where the plant will have what it needs in between visits, such as plant food sticks, automatic watering system, etc.

Step Four - Repeat steps two and three as often as you need through the week.

How Much You Can Earn: This is a very lucrative business, and it is easy to turn this into a top income for your area. Charge according to the number of times you must appear each month and according to the number and type of plants in your care. One such business reported that within a decade of caring for indoor plants for other people, they netted over 3 million dollars. This is a good indication. Part time work can bring in around $15,000 a year, while working this full time can reasonably bring in around $55,000 to $60,000 a year. Work on gaining more clients.

Idea #12 – House Painter

Being a professional house painter requires some knowledge and skill with painting. You can choose from interior or exterior or both. This type of job is easy enough to learn if you have never done it and want to learn how. You may ask a professional house painter if you can be an apprentice under them for a while, or just start by finding people who are willing to allow you to learn how to do it on their home or business. Once you learn the skills this is an in-demand job. You can earn more from this type of job if you become licensed, insured, and bonded. This protects both you and the home owner.

Target Group: Stronger men and women.

Education and Skills Needed: A formal education is not required to be a professional house painter, but you do need both knowledge and skills in painting. You can take courses to help learn the art better. Your best bet would be to start doing this for practice to gain experience. Make sure your own home looks nice and if needed paint both the exterior and interior. Practice on the homes and businesses of family and friends so you can tell potential clients you have a portfolio. Many people will hire someone if they can see their handiwork first.

Where: At the client's home or business.

Equipment Needed: ladders, canvas and plastic drop cloths, paint trays, rollers, paint brushes, painter's tape, face masks, paint sprayer, scaffolding, buckets, towels, sponge brushes, various building materials, plastic wrap, caulk, paint scraper, extension poles, and paint grid.

Step-by-Step for Painting the Exterior of a Home

What to Do: The steps are slightly different, depending on the exterior or interior of the home. Below are steps for each. If you opt to use canvas drop cloths, you can reuse it a lot longer than plastic. While it is initially more expensive, you save in the long run from having to keep purchasing the plastic drop cloths.

Step One - Prep work must come first. You must get rid of dirt, grime, mildew, chipping, and peeling before starting the work. If mildew is present, apply mildew cleaner like a beach and water solution via a sprayer and a hose.

Step Two - Use a pressure washer to blast off the exterior; this will help to loosen and get rid of dirt and leave the surface ready to paint. Allow the exterior to dry completely before moving on to step three.

Step Three - Take a tube of caulk and go around and seal any cracks and cover the joints. Focus around window frames, fascia boards, doorframes, and the molding. Make it as smooth and seamless as possible. Allow the caulk to dry before moving on to step four.

Step Four - Now you will apply primer. Primer sets the surface to hold the new paint to last for years. You will apply the primer the same way you will apply the paint, using a roller or a paintbrush. Completely cover the entire surface where the paint will be applied. Allow to dry and cure before moving on to step five. The primer directions will tell you how long that will take. Be sure to prime any trim areas too.

Step Five - Ask the homeowner if they have picked out the paint. Help them by suggesting a quality brand, exterior acrylic latex paint. They need to pick out both the exterior wall paint and the trim paint.

Step Six - Add the paint to a bucket with a paint grid for faster easier application. This works better than a painter's tray. This works for storage as well; instead of having to clean endless messy trays, just add the lid to the bucket and keep the grid inside. It will be ready for fresh painting the next time.

Step Seven - Determine if you are going to spray, roll, or brush the paint. Most of the largest areas will need to be either rolled or sprayed. Smaller areas will need to be brushed. Add the paint to a 5 gallon bucket and use a paint grid rather than a tray for larger jobs. You will apply one coat over the primer and let it dry before moving on to the optional step eight.

Step Eight - This step is optional. If the first coat of paint covers well, you will not need to apply a second coat. But if the paint does not cover well, you will want to apply a second coat. Allow time to dry before moving on to step nine.

Step Nine - Apply the trim paint to all the trim, molding, and fascia and shutters if applicable. Use painter's tape to keep from bleeding over on the newly-applied paint job. Apply this with smaller rollers and brushes.

Step-by-Step for Painting the Interior of a Home

Step One - Move all furniture away from the walls to be painted. Place drop cloths over furniture and on the floor. As an interior home painter, you need to take extra care in insuring the homeowners' floor and furniture stay clean.

Step Two - Now you do prep work on the walls. You need to clean off any stains first using an all-purpose, vinegar-based cleaner.

Step Three - Scrape any surfaces with peeling paint by using a paint scraper.

Step Four - Repair any holes, cracks, imperfections, and/or dents on the wall with caulk or wall putty. Take time to let it dry and scrape and sand it smooth.

Step Five - Now it's primer time. Once the owner has chosen the paint colors and type of paint (flat, satin, semi-gloss, or high gloss), you will first want to add the primer to the walls. Before painting on the primer, add a small amount of the colored paint to the primer and mix. This will help to bring out the color of the paint and hide stains and imperfections. Some hardware stores will add the color to the primer as well.

Step Six - Start painting the primer with a roller or brush. Avoid the use of a ladder by using an extension pole.

Step Seven - Add the paint to a bucket with a paint grid for faster easier application. This works better than a painter's tray. This works well for storage too; instead of having to clean endless messy trays, just add the lid to the bucket and keep the grid inside. It will be ready for fresh painting the next time.

Step Eight - Add painter's tape to all edges to prevent bleed over.

Step Nine - Apply the paint with sprayers, rollers, and brushes. Allow to dry the proper amount of time as determined from the paint can before applying the second coat.

Step Ten - Once the paint is dry, apply painter's tape around all trim work.

Step Eleven - Paint the trim.

Step Twelve - Clean the mess, remove the drop cloths, and clean all rollers and brushes. Clean the sprayer. Replace the furniture after the paint has dried (if this is a part of your duties).

How Much You Can Earn: Earnings can depend on whether you charge by the hour or by the square foot. It can be hard to give an estimate on time if you are just starting out. For hourly you can charge around $17 to $25 an hour, or charge between $255 and $430 per 100 square feet of area. This includes the price for your equipment. Charge extra if you are purchasing the paint and primer. Most paint jobs take a day or two to complete, so you will earn well over $100 doing this type of work.

Idea #13 – Professional Handyman

Handymen can be men or women who have the special skills to do light carpentry work as well as general home and business maintenance. A true pro will keep up with advances in the field of construction. A handyman can do things as simple as changing light bulbs to adding a room onto the home. You can specify your limitations and do as much or as little as you'd like.

Target Group: Strong men and women.

Education and Skills Needed: Being a professional handyman does not necessarily need a formal education, though there are courses you can take to better your carpentry skills. You do need knowledge and skills for this, either through education or through experience. If you have never done this, you must gain some experience first. You can work for a carpenter or for a construction crew. You need to work with someone who is an expert to learn all the different skills a carpenter knows. This is imperative. Safety is a big concern, so you must familiarize yourself with the proper usage of carpentry tools. Practice by doing carpentry projects on your home. Offer your services to family and friends to help them and gain the vital experience and skills you need in order to be a professional handyman.

Where: At the client's home or business.

Equipment Needed: Being a handyman will have you needing a big variety of tools. Focus on the tools a carpenter needs and start there. Fill a toolbox with the basic tool sets including a hammer, nails, saws, drills and drill bits, wrenches, screwdrivers, and screws. Eventually you will gather items like caulk, putty, and things you will use to repair. With most jobs, the client will purchase the needed materials like lumber, sheetrock, paint, etc.

Steps to Be a Professional Handyman

What to Do: Because a handyman is so diverse, it is difficult to list step-by-step instructions here. Each job will entail different steps. You should only be doing this job if you have the skills as discussed above. Handyman work is plentiful; all you need to do is advertise you are available and the calls will come in, guaranteed.

How Much You Can Earn: As a handyman you can choose to charge a flat fee per job or charge by the hour. If you are well acquainted with the timetable it takes you to do certain jobs, you can make a guesstimate as to the time and adjust it to be a flat fee. Depending on your experience and skillset, you can charge anywhere from $35 to $60 an hour. Charge the client for the cost of actual material used (such as lumber). On average, a handyman may do 6 hour jobs per day, which will net about $210 to $360 earnings per day.

Idea #14 – Tree Cutting/Maintenance

If people have trees in their yard, there will come a time when they will need your services. If you have experience in cutting down trees or in maintaining them, this may be a good business for you. It is not for the faint of heart. A true professional will have the proper equipment (and a place to store it) and will have all the proper bonds and insurance. To be an arborist, you must have some sort of education to learn all the different trees and care of such trees. You can take an arborist course, which is normally just a short, one-week course, to learn what you need to do this job. You will want an International Society of Arboriculture certification as well. You can obtain a state-issued tree maintenance license by contacting your state's Department of Agriculture.

Target Group: Men and women.

Education and Skills Needed: As discussed above, you can take an arborist course to help you gain the knowledge and skills you need to take proper care of trees. The best experience is hands on. Try to meet other professional arborists and tree cutters and learn through hands-on work.

Where: At the client's home or business.

Equipment Needed: saws, chainsaws, ladders, safety gear, a rigging system, stump grinders, pruning shears, rigging rope, steel-toed boots, and pulleys.

Steps to Be a Tree Cutter/Tree Maintainer (Arborist)

What to Do: This is a varied job. Your work will be dependent upon the type of trees you are maintaining or cutting down. It is important that you know what you are doing. Take the advice above and educate yourself on the proper care of such trees through the International Society of Arboriculture.

How Much You Can Earn: A certified tree arborist can earn up to $50,000 a year or more when working the business full time. That's almost $200 a day. The average falls somewhere between $100 to $200 a day.

Ideas that Require Special Skills

These are job ideas that you can do if you possess the passion to do these things. Each one requires special skills and special equipment. If you don't care for these things you should move on. You will only be able to do these if you enjoy doing them first as a hobby.

Idea #15 – Outdoor Photographer

An outdoor photographer does not have the need for special equipment aside from a good camera and perhaps a tripod. Outdoor photos use natural lighting to create the best images. Family portraits have morphed into more natural poses which take place outside. This is a new and booming business if you are handy with a good camera.

Target Group: Men and women who have a love for photography.

Education and Skills Needed: You can take courses in photography and even work to gain a degree, though it's not necessary. This is a special skill and you need to know the camera and how to take very good photos. You cannot just pick up a camera and charge fees to people to snap their portraits without having skills and knowledge about what you are doing.

Practice is your second best bet in learning the trade. Practice on your own family and friends. Offer to do family portraits for a church group or non-profit group to help them. This gives you experience. The more you practice the better you will become.

Where: Anywhere picturesque outside.

Equipment Needed: A good, high-megapixel camera with the ability to zoom and use manual focus, polarizing filters, telephoto zoom lens, tripod, umbrella, camera bag, and props.

Steps to Being an Outdoor Photographer

What to Do: This is a wide-open option; you can take the photos wherever you feel would be good. These steps are just suggestions, as this section is more for the person who is already an expert.

These steps are in no particular order.

- Choose a time of day that the sunlight will not be in the eyes of the subjects.
- Any place can be a photo opportunity: nature scenes such as in grass, in the forest, by a creek, at a lake, at the beach, or at a park. Or city type scenes, on a street, with an old building in the background. Or out in the country, have a barn in the background, or an old house, a well, or a garden.

The possibilities are endless for outdoor backdrops. Use your imagination to see what you can come up with.

- Photograph sports teams, the teams and the individuals.
- Photograph family portraits using the above suggestions for backdrops.
- Photograph children.
- Photograph special occasions outside. Prom, graduation, senior pictures, first dance, religious ceremonies like first communion, confirmation, baptism, etc.
- Photograph family reunions/generations.
- Ask hospitals to put a flyer in with new baby going home gifts.

- Put in bids with the local schools to be the outdoor sports photographer.
- Advertise in the local papers and radio stations.
- Put flyers up at store bulletin boards.
- Word of mouth; spread the word.
- Give referral gifts to people who bring you clients such as a free 8x10 or keychain.

How Much You Can Earn: Photographers today have it easier than those of the yesterday years. To be quick and easy, do a family portrait session and charge a flat fee. Have the family give you a flash drive and put all the images in digital form on the flash drive. You walk away with the entire fee and it only costs you your time. If you offer packages, having prints made is very inexpensive. You can go to your local discount department store or build an account online if you wish. You can offer package deals for an average of $50 for sports packages. You will pocket around $35 to $40 per package. Charge flat fees for family portrait sessions. If you are simply giving back a flash drive, you can charge anywhere from $100 to $300 per session. If you are giving prints, add to the fee.

Idea #16 – Baker/Cook

While being a baker is something you can do with a restaurant or specialty store, you can also offer your services right from your own kitchen. If you enjoy cooking and baking, you can offer to cater meals or make cakes, cookies, pies, and other special food items.

Target Group: Women and men who love to bake and or cook.

Education and Skills Needed: You do need special skills to be a good baker and cook. You can take courses and even attend college to gain a degree towards this. Learn all you can about how to be the best baker and cook. Take courses and/or watch tutorials on TV and YouTube. Practice makes perfect, so cook for your family, and cook for your friends. Offer to help out with parties and events to gain the experience. Take a lot of photos of your work. People love to see what you can do. Take a photo of the finished product. And keep practicing.

Where: From your own kitchen, delivered to your client (or the client can pick it up).

Equipment Needed: bowls, spatulas, spoons, forks, cake pans of all sizes, springform pans, pie pans of all sizes, baking dishes, baking sheets, electric mixer, cake decorating tools, cookie cutters, oven(s), food necessary to make the special baked items or cooked foods, disposable pans, and cupcake papers.

Steps in Being a Baker/Cook

What to Do: As a special skill job such as this, the steps will vary according to what you are cooking/baking. These are general steps and suggestions to make this line of work profitable.

- Advertise in your local paper, local radio station, and flyers on store bulletin boards
- Go to businesses that allow for other business cards and leave a stack advertising what you offer
- Help to spread the word by donating baked goods to various bake sales
- Offer to make birthday cakes and celebration cakes
- Target wedding shops for bridal and wedding showers
- Target maternity and baby shops for baby showers

Guaranteed Ways to Make $100 Today - Legally

- Target toy stores for birthday parties
- Start with a specialty item such as cupcakes or cakes
- Offer to cater family reunions, parties, gatherings
- Ask a store if you can set up a free sample booth to display your goods and hand out flyers

How Much You Can Earn: You need to calculate how much time it takes to make a food item and calculate the cost of the food and the energy required to cook it to come up with your fees. You would want to charge set fees per food item rather than an hourly fee. This works best for freelance bakers. For example, if it takes you 2 hours to bake and frost a cake, you can charge anywhere from $15-$20 per hour for your time and for the amount of the ingredients. Say it costs $10 in food and 2 hours of your time to make a batch of cupcakes, charge $40 to 45 for the cupcakes or the cake. If you can gather 2 to 3 orders a day for this, you can easily make over $100 a day. Word of mouth goes a long way in this business if you do a good job. People love to eat and a good cook is worth the extra fee.

Idea #17 – Seamstress

Believe it or not, there are still needs for seamstresses these days. People purchase clothing that doesn't quite fit; they may need a hem taken up or let out. They may need buttons sewn on or a minor repair. People are busy and normally do not have time for such minor sewing jobs. Also there is still a need for specialty sewing. Women love exclusive wedding gowns. Create uniforms, costumes, and other special items. You can also create unique items to sell on eBay or Etsy. This job requires a person with good skills with a sewing machine and needle and thread. You need to be skilled in operating a sewing machine and know how to use patterns.

Target Group: Women and men who love to sew.

Education and Skills Needed: No formal education is required to be a seamstress, but you do need to possess the skills to do the sewing tasks. The best way to learn this craft is through hands-on training. You can take courses and classes to learn how to sew. The best thing you can do is to practice by sewing your own clothing, mending, and repairing. Offer to do so for family and friends. Offer your services for free while training to groups who may need uniforms or costumes. Once you gain experience, you will have enough skills to be able to charge others for your services. Take photos of your creations to use as a portfolio.

Where: At your home at your sewing machine.

Equipment Needed: Sewing machine, large table, pins, pin cushion, needles, threads of all colors, buttons, fabric, patterns, seam tape, scissors (various sizes), ironing board, and iron.

Steps in Being a Seamstress

What to Do: This job requires a varied amount of steps, depending on the request. Below will be a basic outline and advice on making this a profitable business.

- Advertise your business on the local radio and in the local paper. Add flyers to store bulletin boards.
- Talk with the local school about offering to sew special uniforms and costumes for clubs and teams.
- Offer to sew special outfits for special occasions, parties, weddings, etc.
- Offer to mend and repair clothing.
- Acquire a special sewing machine that does embroidery and offer personalized clothing and fabric items.

How Much You Can Earn: Basically, you will want to charge an hourly rate plus the cost of the materials. The rates are anywhere from $15 to $25 an hour, depending on your skills level. If you are creating a wedding dress that takes 20 hours to sew, you can charge $500 plus the cost of the materials. Try to judge each job according to how long it will take you to finish it. For small jobs such as hemming trousers, charge a flat fee of $10 to $20. You can easily earn over $100 a day if you gather enough work.

Final Words

Now that you've read through the job ideas, you are bound to have some ideas of your own. All the advice and steps here serve to help you figure out what you can do to earn a decent day's wage. You can earn more or less depending on your area, your expertise level, your experience, your education, and your willingness to work hard.

You will want to work hard for your clients. Give more than 100% of your effort. Go the extra mile. Deliver more than their money's worth. Why? Because this shows you have integrity. The "pay it forward" theory will come back to reward you tenfold when your happy and satisfied clients will sing your praises to everyone they know. This is what sparks good word of mouth. Happy clients are the lifeblood of your business, and you will want to keep them that way.

Actual results and earnings depend on your experience and skills and the going rates in your area for the job you choose. The more you learn how to do the work better, improving your skills, and gaining more experience, the greater the bottom line will be. Hard work and honest effort pays off well. Keep integrity first in all of your business dealings. Always treat your client in the same way you wish to be treated. Keep your word. If you say you will show up at a certain time then make sure you show up. If you are going to be running late, give your client a call to let them know. It shows good will on your part if you show up a little early and stay a little late, especially if you are just starting the business.

You can even combine businesses if you wish. People can offer, for example, aquarium maintenance with indoor plant care. Many of the jobs are easily combined. Use your imagination and enjoy what you do!

www.ingramcontent.com/pod-product-compliance
Lightning Source LLC
Chambersburg PA
CBHW051537170526
45165CB00002B/774